EASY PIANO

THE BEATLES
SONGS IN EASY KEYS

"The Beatles in Easy Keys" include no more than one sharp or one flat in the **key signature**.
The key signature appears on the left side of every staff, right next to the clef signs.

no sharps or flats

one sharp: F#
all Fs are played as F#

one flat: B♭
all Bs are played as B♭

Sometimes **accidentals** appear. Accidentals are sharps and flats not in the key signature.
An accidental alters a specific note in a particular measure. The next bar line or a
natural sign (♮) cancels an accidental.

F# (in key signature)

F♮

ISBN 978-1-70518-817-0

HAL•LEONARD®
7777 W. BLUEMOUND RD. P.O. BOX 13819 MILWAUKEE, WI 53213

Visit Hal Leonard Online at
www.halleonard.com

World headquarters, contact:
Hal Leonard
7777 West Bluemound Road
Milwaukee, WI 53213
Email: info@halleonard.com

In Europe, contact:
Hal Leonard Europe Limited
1 Red Place
London, W1K 6PL
Email: info@halleonardeurope.com

In Australia, contact:
Hal Leonard Australia Pty. Ltd.
4 Lentara Court
Cheltenham, Victoria, 3192 Australia
Email: info@halleonard.com.au

ALL MY LOVING

Words and Music by JOHN LENNON
and PAUL McCARTNEY

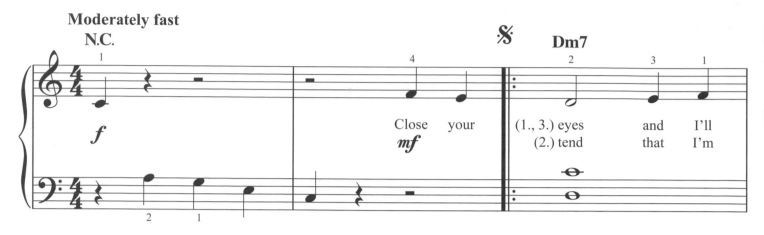

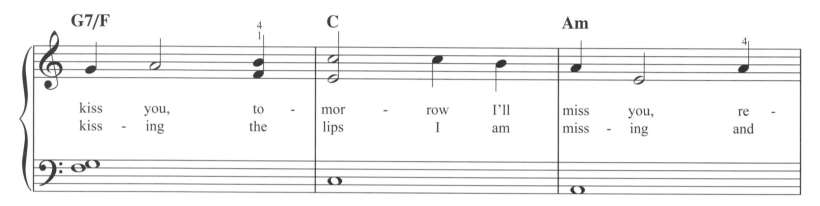

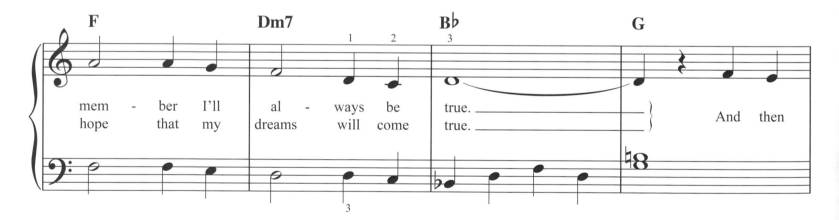

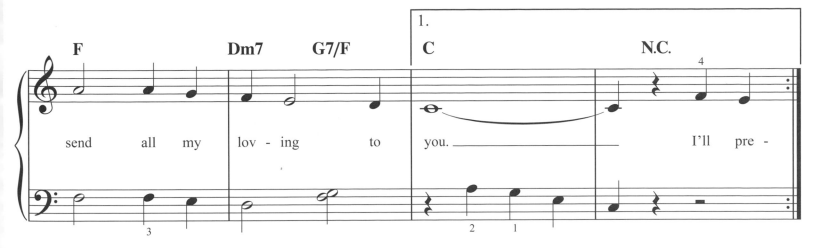

F   **Dm7**   **G7/F**   **1.** **C**   **N.C.**

send   all   my   lov - ing   to   you.   I'll pre -

2., 3. **C**   **N.C.**   **Am**   **G#+**

you.   All   my   lov - ing,   I   will   send   to

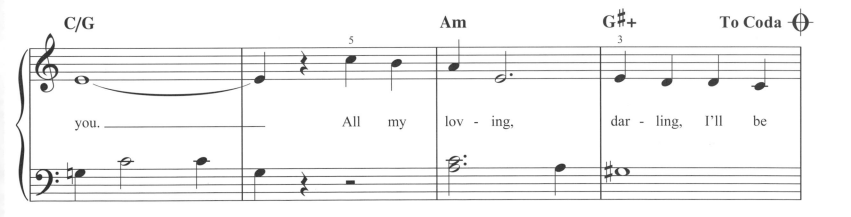

C/G   **Am**   **G#+**   **To Coda** ⊕

you.   All   my   lov - ing,   dar - ling, I'll be

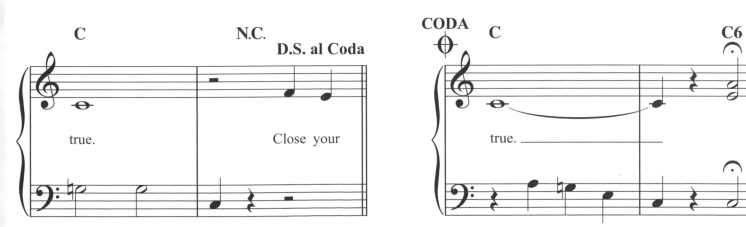

C   **N.C.**   **CODA** ⊕ **C**   **C6**
                D.S. al Coda

true.   Close your   true.

AND I LOVE HER

Words and Music by JOHN LENNON
and PAUL McCARTNEY

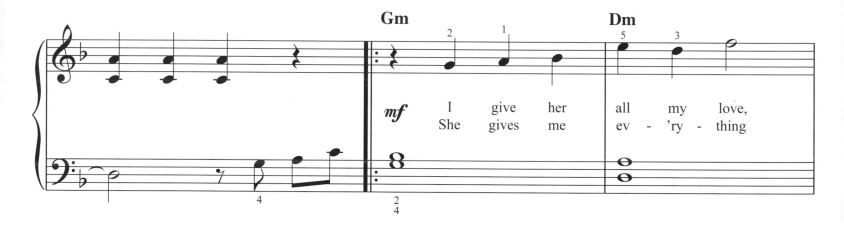

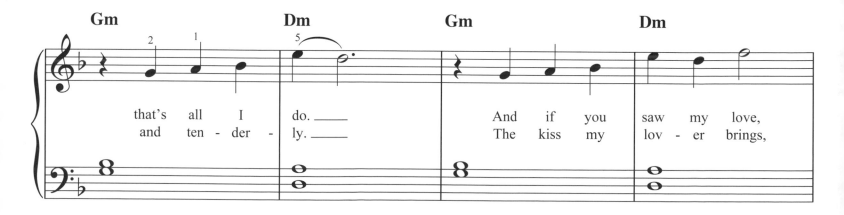

you'd love her   too. ___   I ___   love   her. ___
she brings to   me. ___   And I   love   her. ___

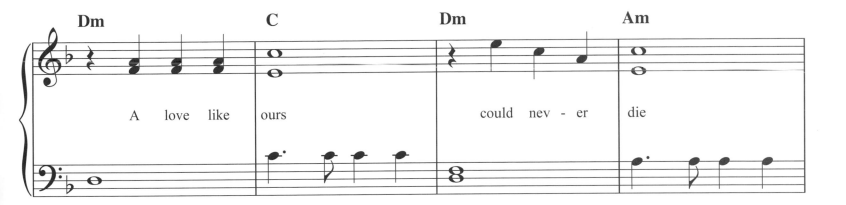

A   love   like   ours   could   nev - er   die

as   long   as   I   have   you   near   me. ___

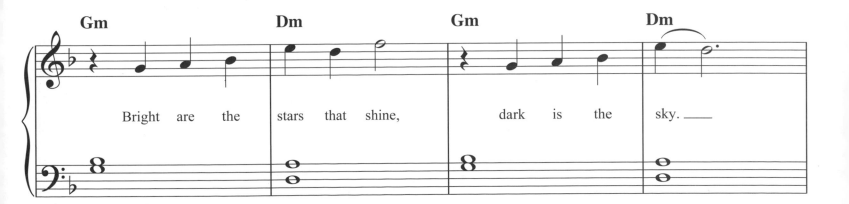

Bright   are   the   stars   that   shine,   dark   is   the   sky. ___

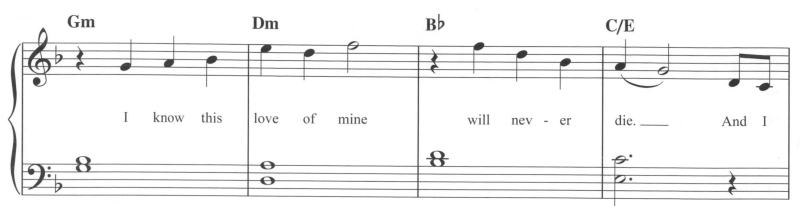

I know this love of mine will nev - er die. _____ And I

love her. _____

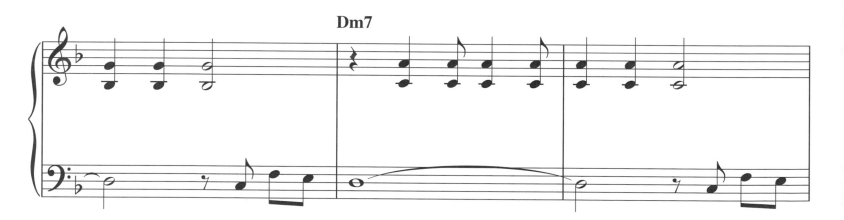

ALL YOU NEED IS LOVE

Words and Music by JOHN LENNON
and PAUL McCARTNEY

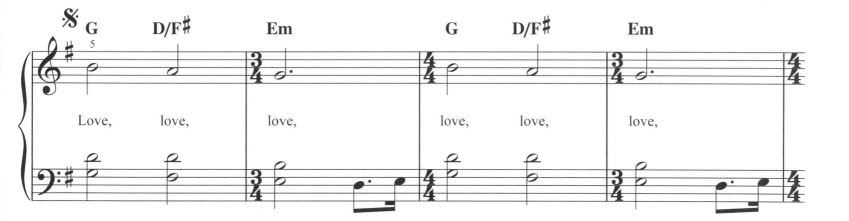

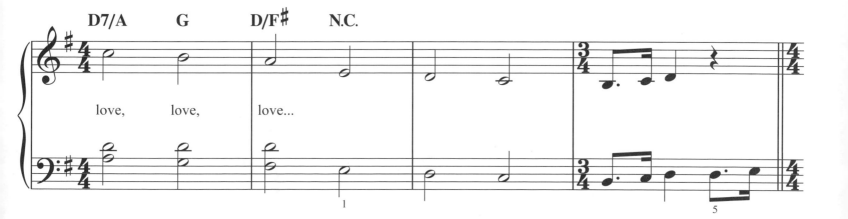

There's noth - ing you can do that can't be done.
Noth - ing you can make that can't be made.
Noth - ing you can know that is - n't known.

Noth - ing you can sing that can't be sung.
No one you can save that can't be saved.
Noth - ing you can see that is - n't shown.

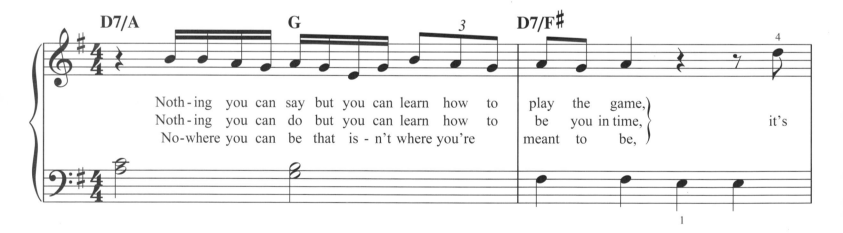

Noth - ing you can say but you can learn how to play the game,)
Noth - ing you can do but you can learn how to be you in time,} it's
No-where you can be that is - n't where you're meant to be,)

eas - y.

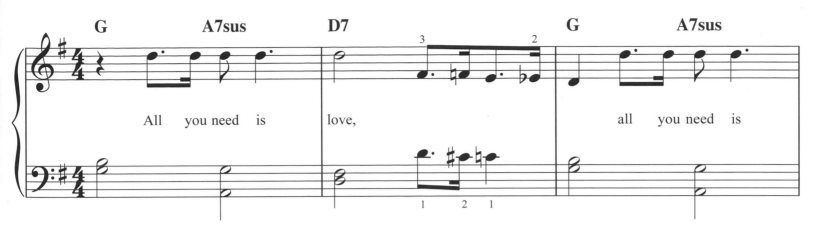

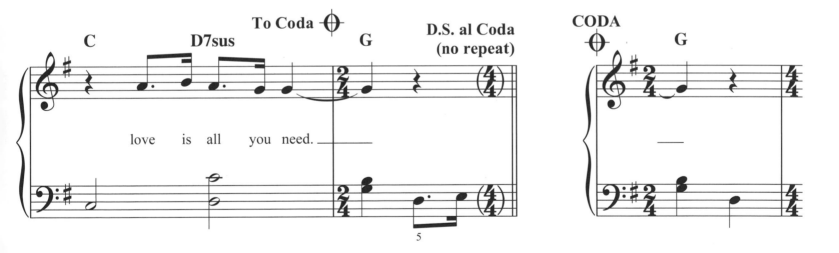

CAN'T BUY ME LOVE

Words and Music by JOHN LENNON
and PAUL McCARTNEY

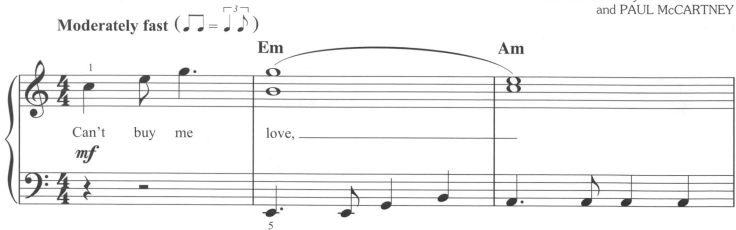

thing, my friend, if it makes you feel al - right.)
lot to give, but what I've got I'll give to you.) 'Cause

I don't care too much for mon - ey, mon - ey can't buy me

love. I'll love. Can't buy me love, _____

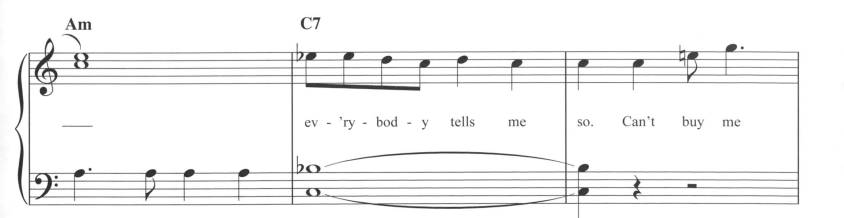

_____ ev - 'ry - bod - y tells me so. Can't buy me

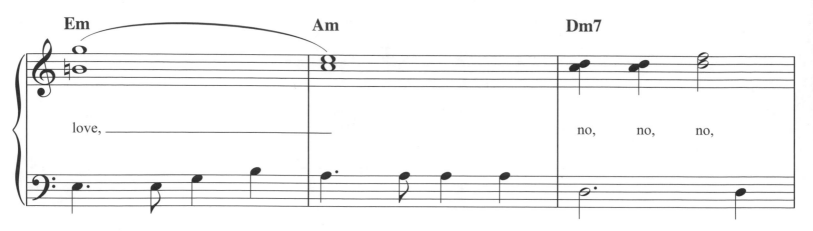

Em   **Am**   **Dm7**

love,   no,   no,   no,

G   **C7**   3

no!   Say   you   don't   need   no   dia - mond   rings   and

I'll   be   sat - is -   fied.   **F7**   Tell   me   that   you   want   the

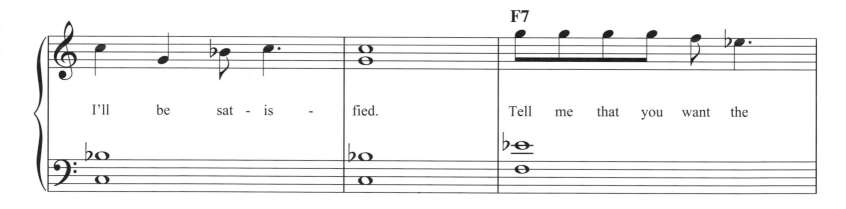

C7

kind   of   things   that   mon - ey   just   can't   buy.

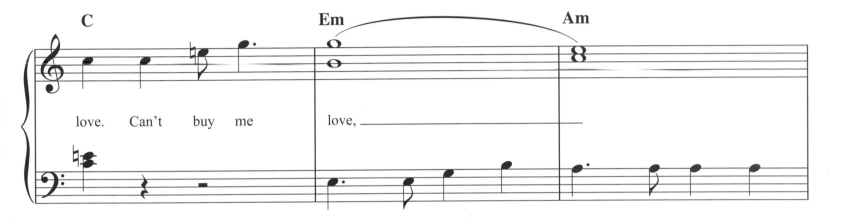

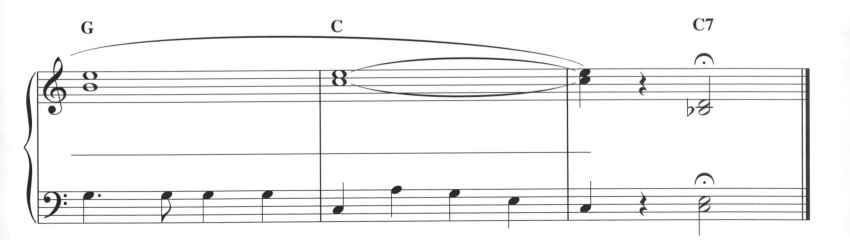

DO YOU WANT TO KNOW A SECRET?

Words and Music by JOHN LENNON
and PAUL McCARTNEY

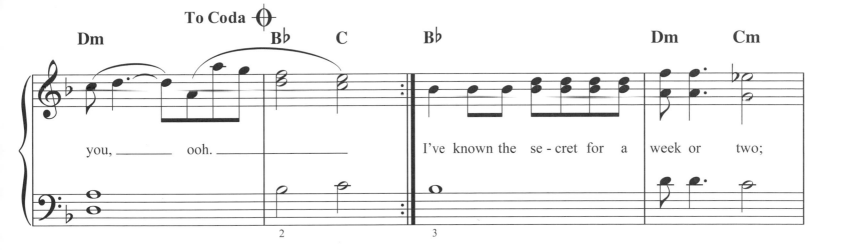

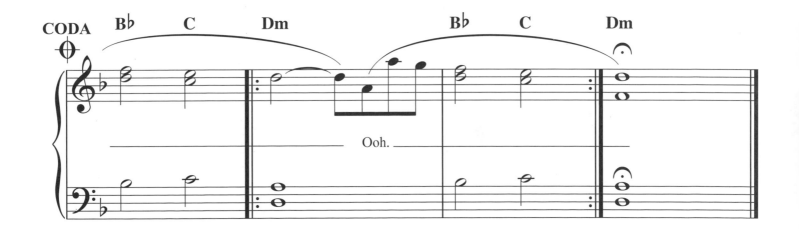

ELEANOR RIGBY

Words and Music by JOHN LENNON
and PAUL McCARTNEY

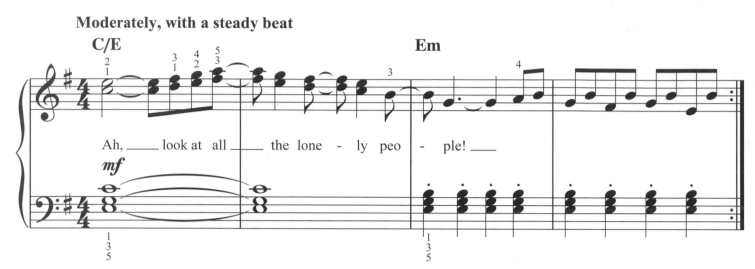

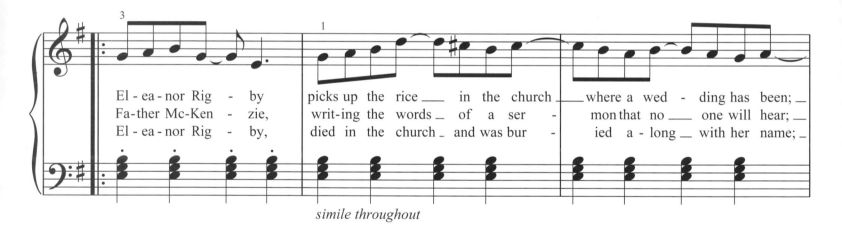

wear-ing the face __ that she keeps __ in a jar __ by the door; __
darn-ing his socks __ in the night __ when there's no - bod - y there; __
wip-ing the dirt __ from his hands __ as he walks __ from the grave; __

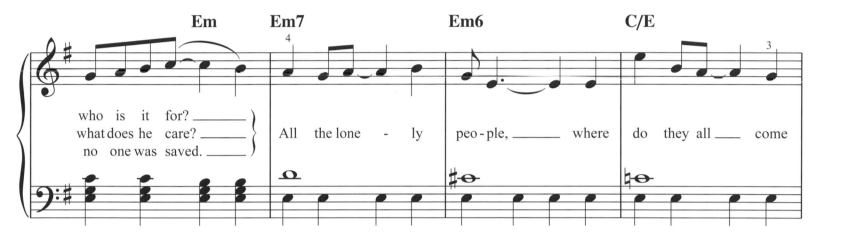

Em **Em7** **Em6** **C/E**

who is it for? _____
what does he care? _____
no one was saved. _____

All the lone - ly peo - ple, _____ where do they all __ come

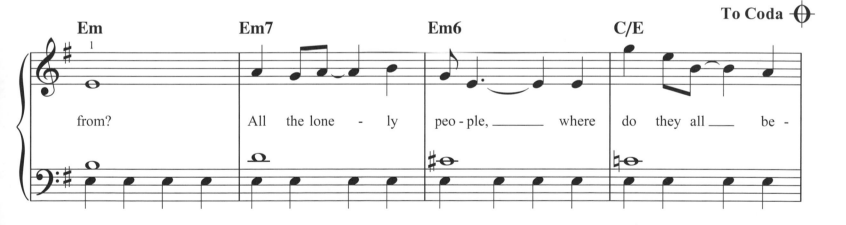

Em **Em7** **Em6** **C/E** **To Coda**

from? All the lone - ly peo - ple, _____ where do they all __ be -

1.
Em

long?

2.
Em **D.C. al Coda**

long?

CODA
Em

long?
rit.

GOLDEN SLUMBERS

Words and Music by JOHN LENNON
and PAUL McCARTNEY

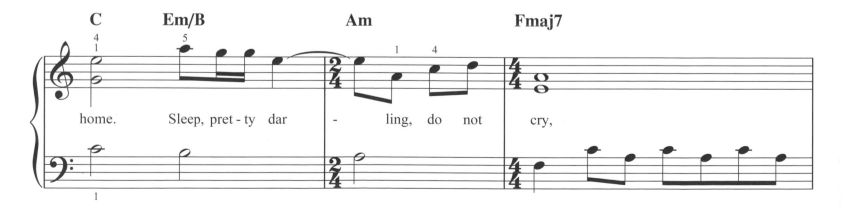

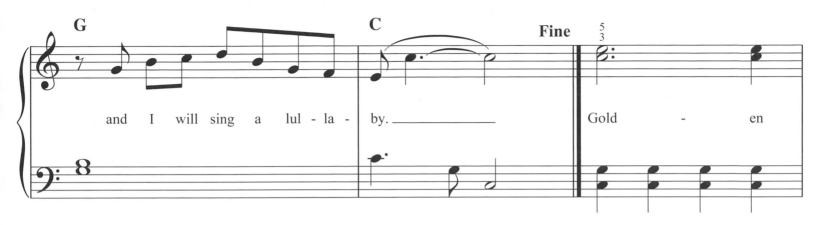

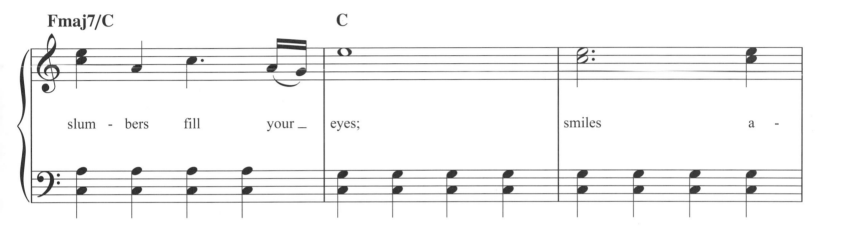

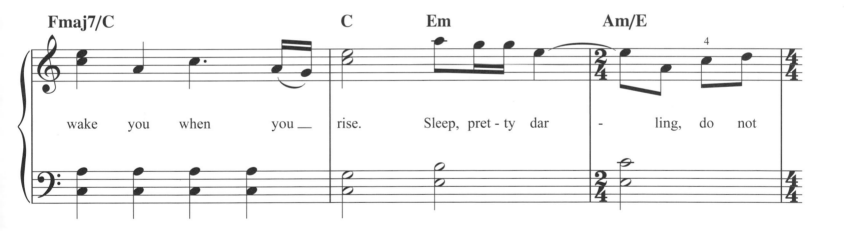

GOOD DAY SUNSHINE

Words and Music by JOHN LENNON
and PAUL McCARTNEY

Good day ___ sun - shine, ___ good day ___ sun - shine, ___

good day ___ sun - shine.

{ I need to laugh and when the
Then we'd lie be - neath a

sun is out,   I've got some-thing I can   laugh a - bout. ___ I feel
shad - y tree,   I love her ___ and she's   lov - ing me. ___ She feels

good _____ in a spe-cial way, _____ I'm in love, and it's a
good, ____ she knows she's look-ing fine, _____ I'm so proud to know that

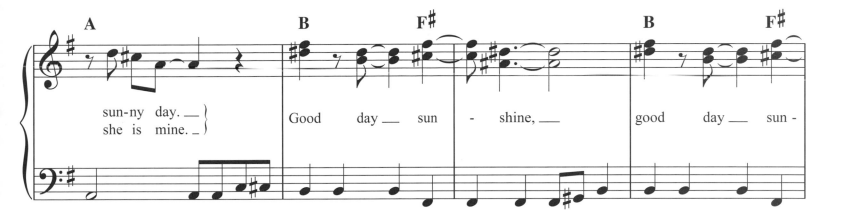

sun-ny day. ____ }
she is mine. ____ } Good day ____ sun - shine, ____ good day ____ sun-

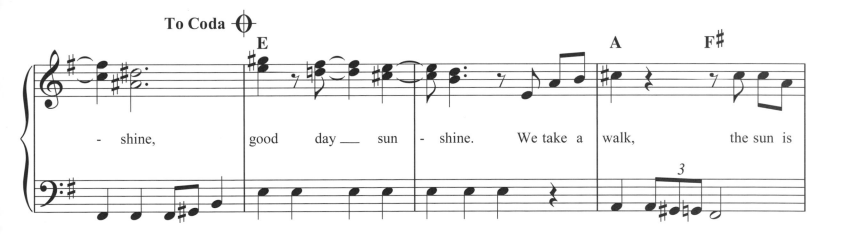

To Coda ⊕

- shine, _____ good day ____ sun - shine. We take a walk, _____ the sun is

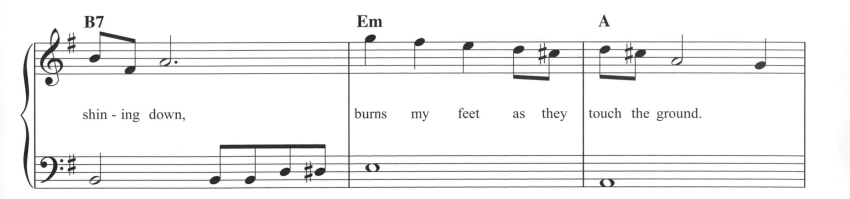

shin - ing down, _____ burns my feet as they touch the ground.

good day ___ sun - shine. Good day ___ sun -

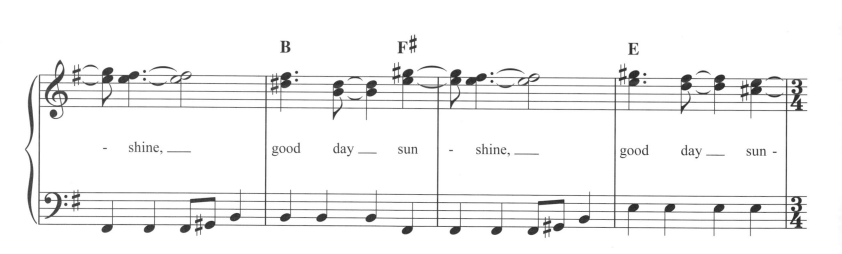

- shine, ___ good day ___ sun - shine, ___ good day ___ sun -

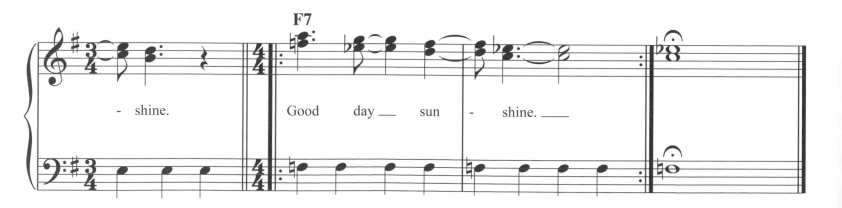

- shine. Good day ___ sun - shine. ___

HERE COMES THE SUN

Words and Music by
GEORGE HARRISON

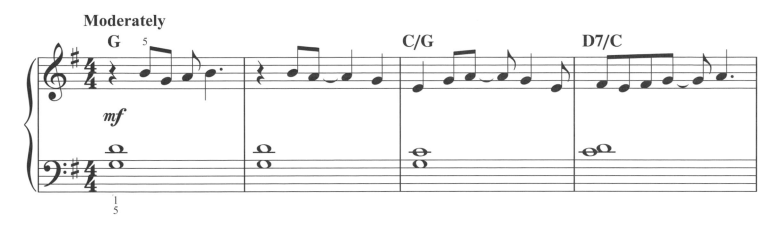

sun, and I say, "It's all right."

1., 2.

3.

"It's all right."

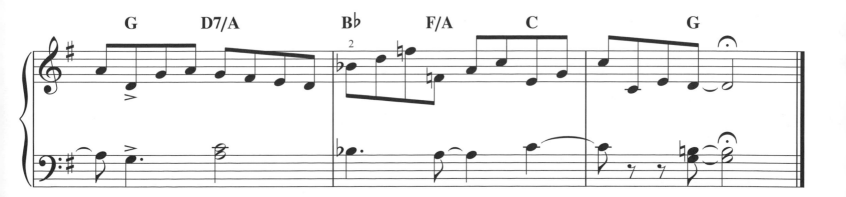

GOOD NIGHT

Words and Music by JOHN LENNON
and PAUL McCARTNEY

Slowly and dreamily

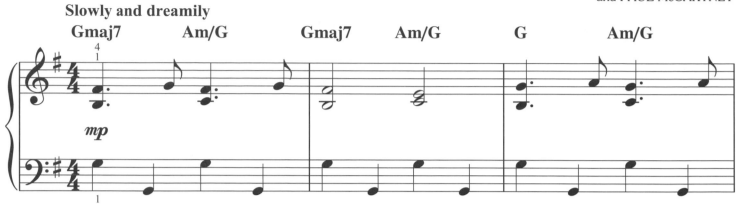

Now it's time to say good night. Good night,

sleep tight. Now the sun turns out his light.

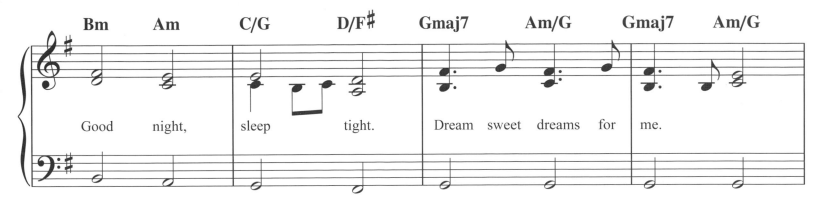

Good night, sleep tight. Dream sweet dreams for me.

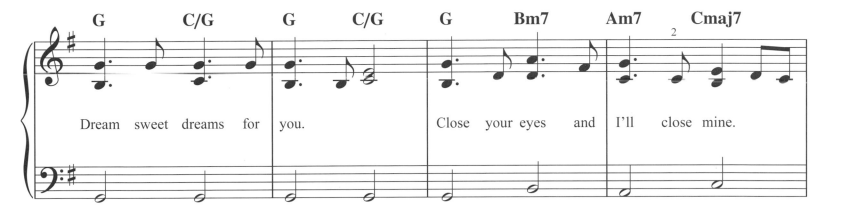

Dream sweet dreams for you. Close your eyes and I'll close mine.

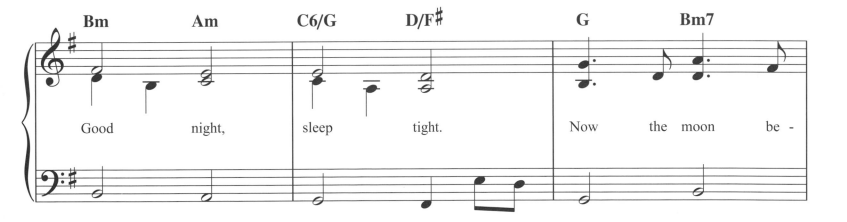

Good night, sleep tight. Now the moon be -

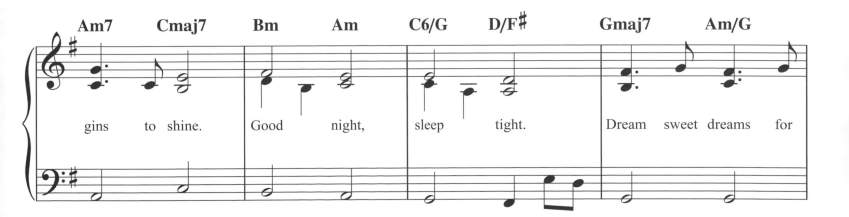

gins to shine. Good night, sleep tight. Dream sweet dreams for

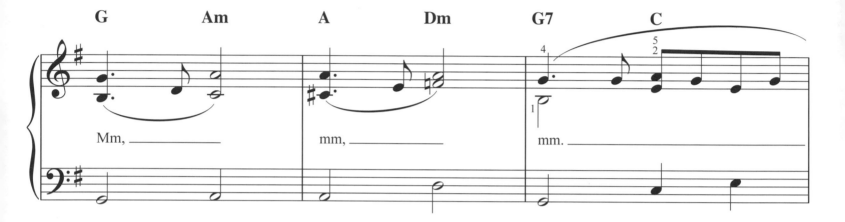

out his light. Good night, sleep tight.

Dream sweet dreams for me, dream sweet dreams for

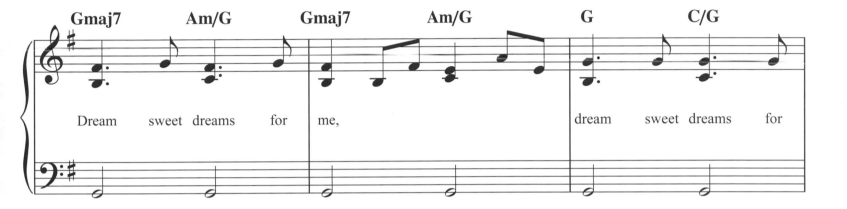

you. *(Whispered:) Good night.*

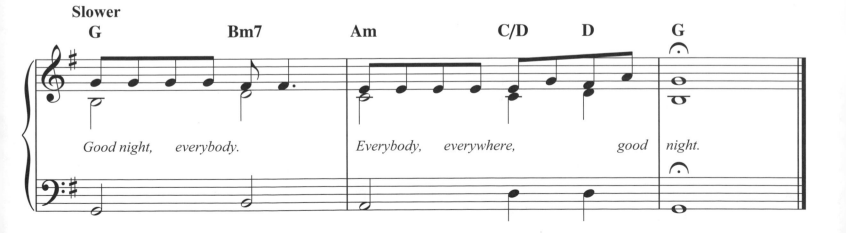

Slower

Good night, everybody. Everybody, everywhere, good night.

HEY JUDE

Words and Music by JOHN LENNON
and PAUL McCARTNEY

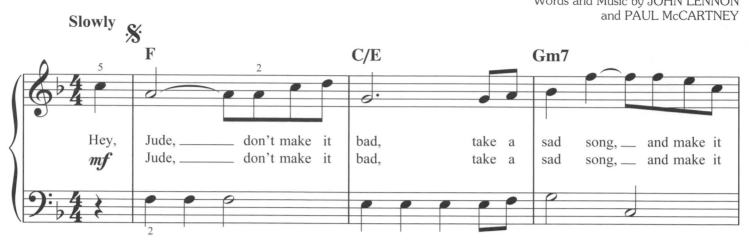

min - ute you let her un - der your skin, then you be - gin ___
mem - ber to let her in - to your heart; then you can start ___

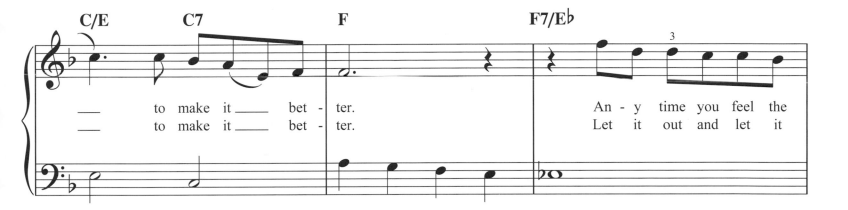

___ to make it ___ bet - ter. An - y time you feel the
___ to make it ___ bet - ter. Let it out and let it

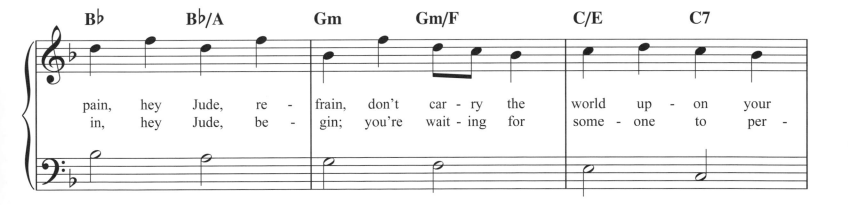

pain, hey Jude, re - frain, don't car - ry the world up - on your
in, hey Jude, be - gin; you're wait - ing for some - one to per -

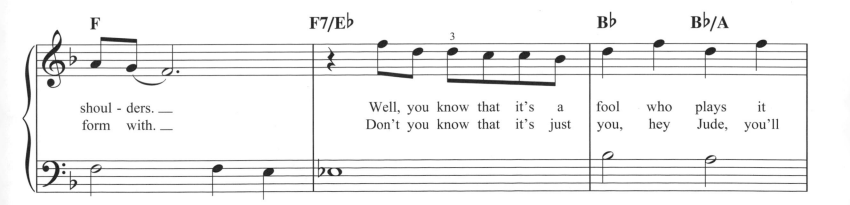

shoul - ders. ___ Well, you know that it's a fool who plays it
form with. ___ Don't you know that it's just you, hey Jude, you'll

cool, by mak - ing his world a lit - tle cold - er. ⏤ } Da da
do, the move-ment you need is on your shoul - der. ⏤ }

da da da da da da. Hey
da. Hey

D.S. al Coda

CODA

ter. Da da da da da da da

da da da da hey ⏤ Jude.
Jude.

STRAWBERRY FIELDS FOREVER

Words and Music by JOHN LENNON
and PAUL McCARTNEY

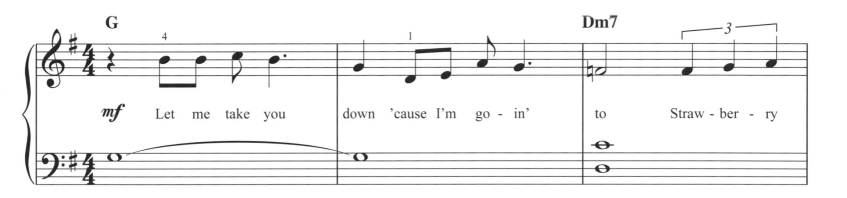

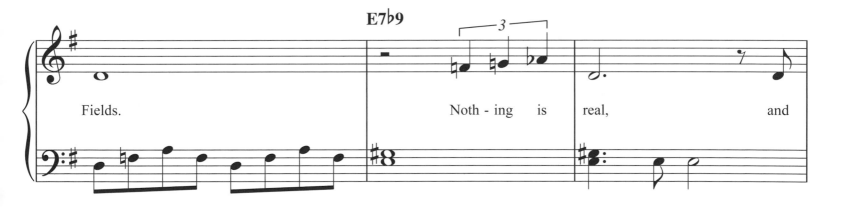

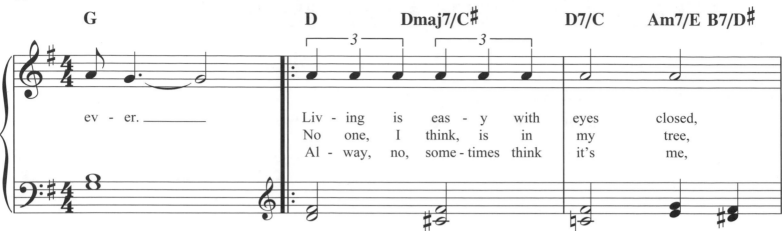

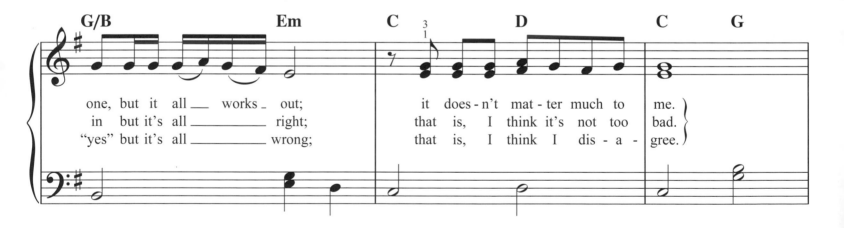

Noth-ing is real, and noth-ing to get hung a-bout.

Straw-ber - ry Fields _ for - ev - er. _____

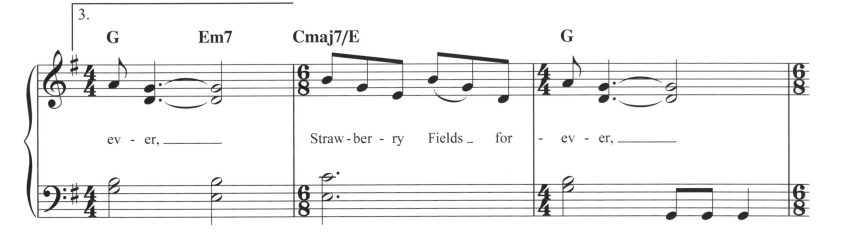

ev - er, _____ Straw-ber - ry Fields _ for - ev - er, _____

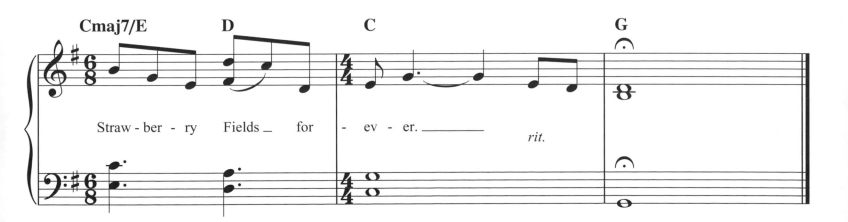

Straw - ber - ry Fields _ for - ev - er. _____

I AM THE WALRUS

Words and Music by JOHN LENNON
and PAUL McCARTNEY

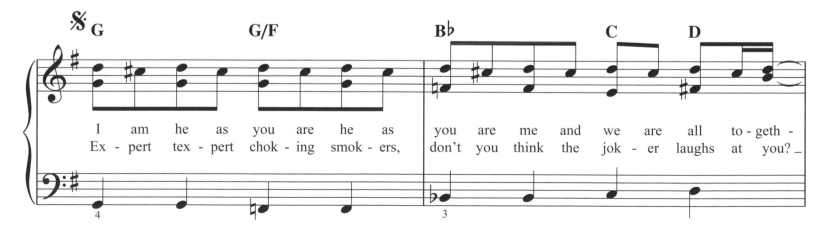

I am he as you are he as you are me and we are all to-geth-
Ex-pert tex-pert chok-ing smok-ers, don't you think the jok-er laughs at you? _

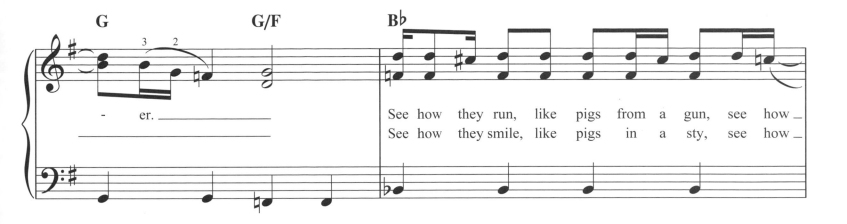

See how they run, like pigs from a gun, see how
See how they smile, like pigs in a sty, see how

they fly. I'm cry - ing.
they snied. I'm cry - ing.

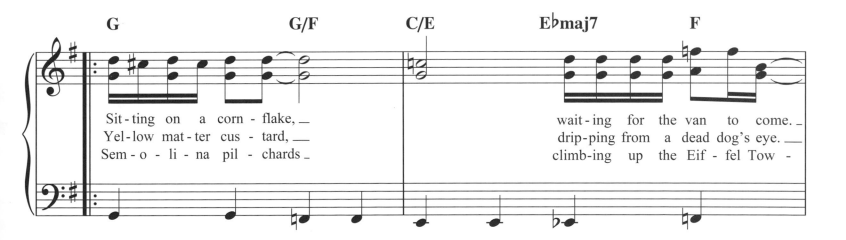

Sit - ting on a corn - flake, wait - ing for the van to come.
Yel - low mat - ter cus - tard, drip - ping from a dead dog's eye.
Sem - o - li - na pil - chards climb - ing up the Eif - fel Tow -

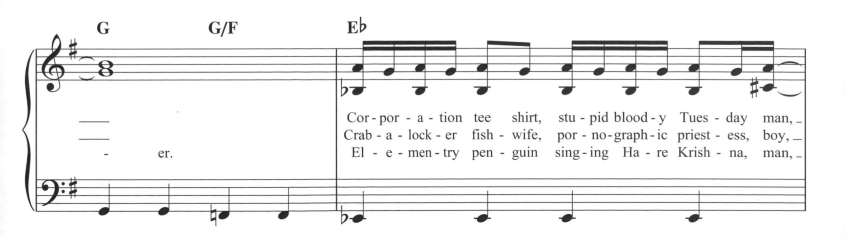

- er. Cor - por - a - tion tee shirt, stu - pid blood - y Tues - day man,
Crab - a - lock - er fish - wife, por - no - graph - ic priest - ess, boy,
El - e - men - try pen - guin sing - ing Ha - re Krish - na, man,

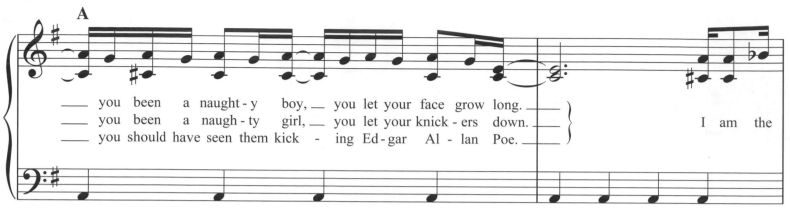

A

__ you been a naught-y boy, __ you let your face grow long. __
__ you been a naugh-ty girl, __ you let your knick-ers down. __
__ you should have seen them kick-ing Ed-gar Al-lan Poe. __

I am the

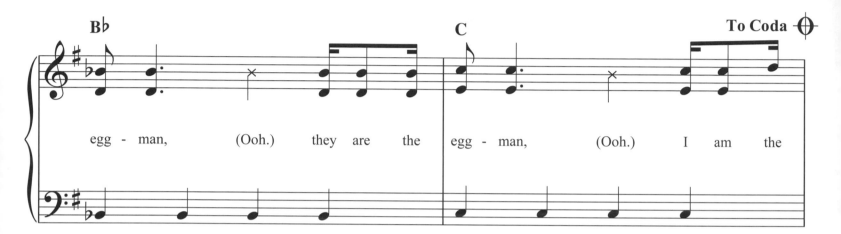

B♭   **C**   **To Coda** ⊕

egg-man,   (Ooh.)   they are the   egg-man,   (Ooh.)   I am the

D

1.
G   **G/F**

wal-rus.   Goo goo g' joob.   Mis-ter cit-y p'lice-man sit-ting

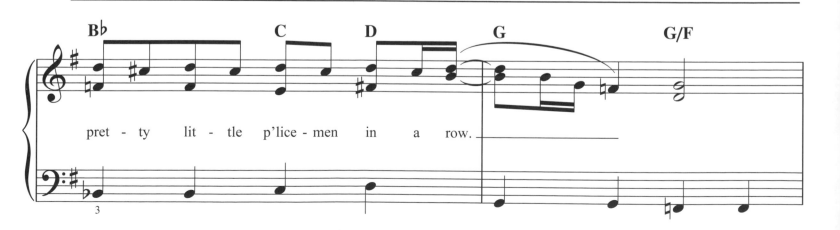

B♭   **C**   **D**   **G**   **G/F**

pret-ty lit-tle p'lice-men in a row. __

3

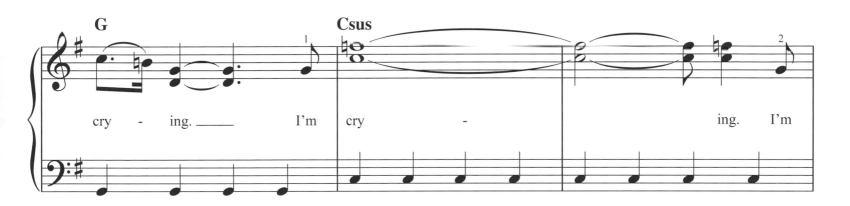

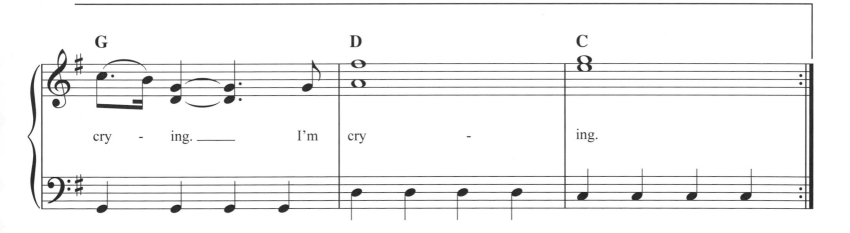

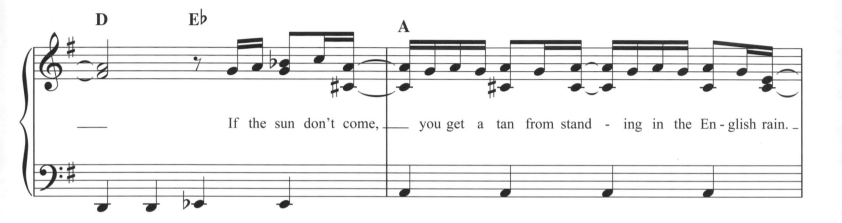

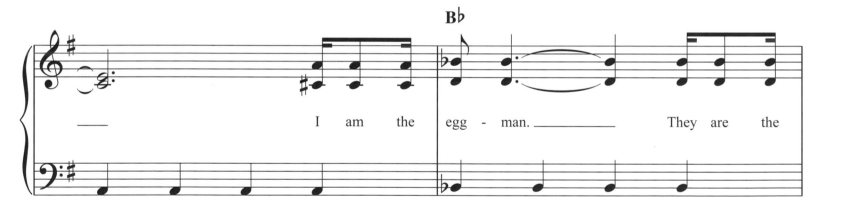

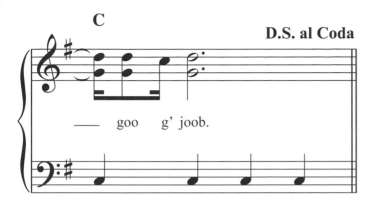

D.S. al Coda

goo g' joob.

CODA

wal - rus. Goo goo g' joob, g' goo

goo g' joob.

Goo goo g' goo g' goo ___ goo g' joob

joob.

Optional Ending

Repeat and Fade

I'LL FOLLOW THE SUN

Words and Music by JOHN LENNON
and PAUL McCARTNEY

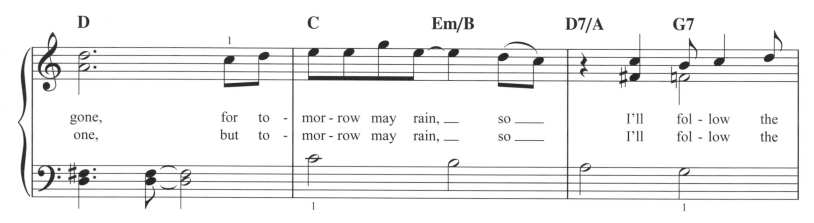

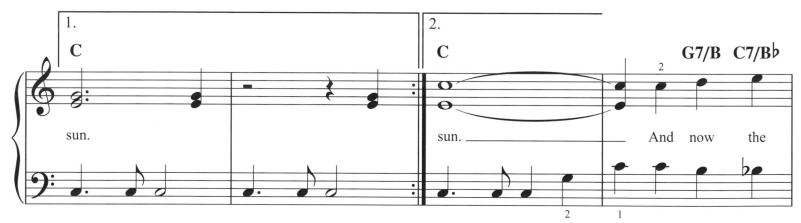

And though I lose a friend __ in the end __ you will

know, oh. __ One day __ you'll find __

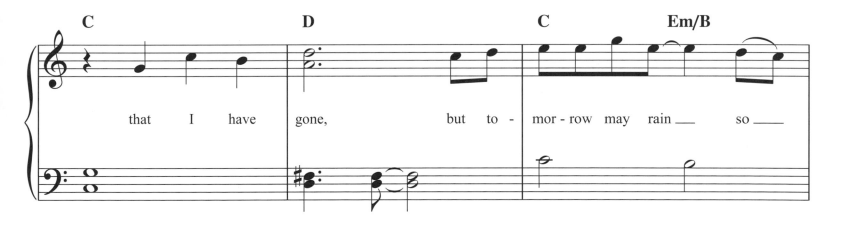

that I have gone, but to - mor - row may rain __ so __

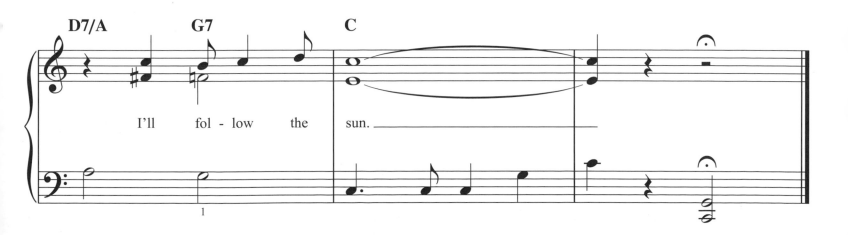

I'll fol - low the sun. __

IN MY LIFE

Words and Music by JOHN LENNON
and PAUL McCARTNEY

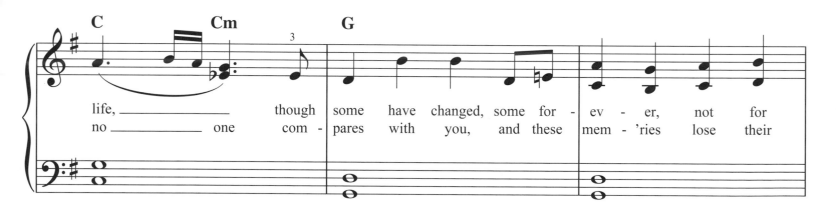

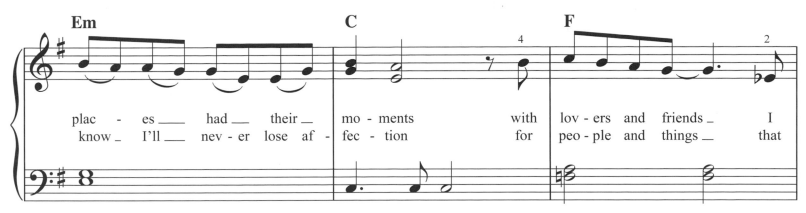

plac–es ____ had ____ their ____ | mo – ments | with | lov – ers and friends ____ | I
know ____ I'll ____ nev – er lose af – | fec – tion | for | peo – ple and things ____ | that

still can re – call. ____ Some are | dead ____ and ____ some ____ are ____
went ____ be – fore, ____ I | know I'll of – ten stop and think a –

liv – ing. In | my _____ life, I've | loved them all. ____
bout them. In | my _____ life, I | love you more. ____

rit.

LET IT BE

Words and Music by JOHN LENNON
and PAUL McCARTNEY

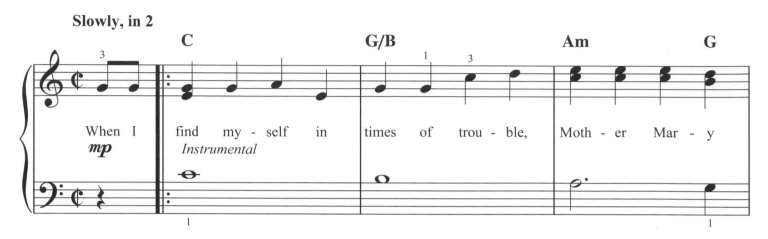

When I find my-self in times of trou-ble, Moth-er Mar-y

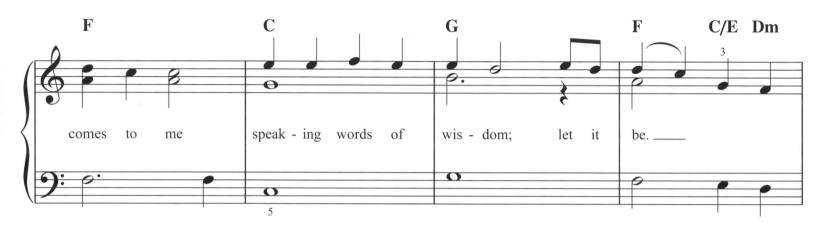

comes to me speak-ing words of wis-dom; let it be.

And in my hour of dark-ness she is stand-ing right in

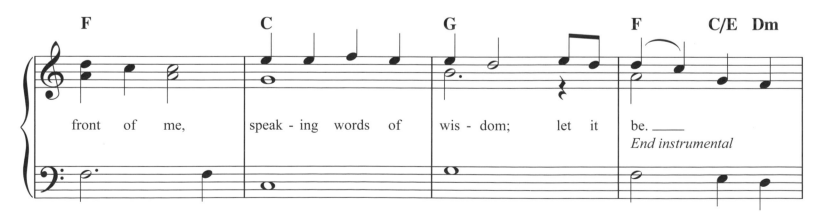

front of me, speak-ing words of wis-dom; let it be.

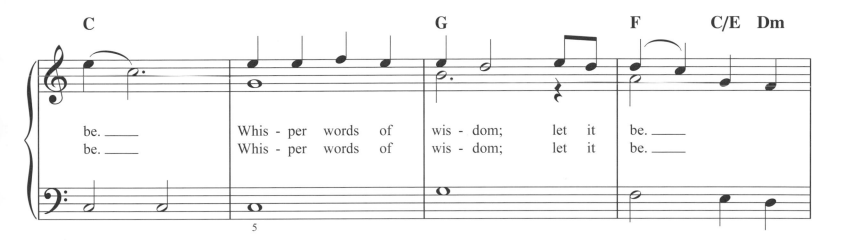

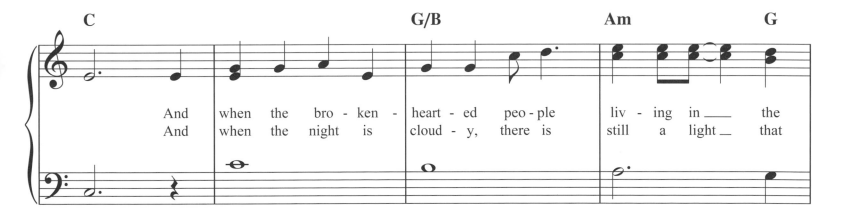

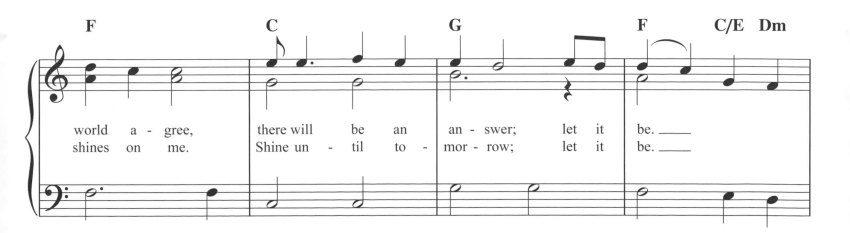

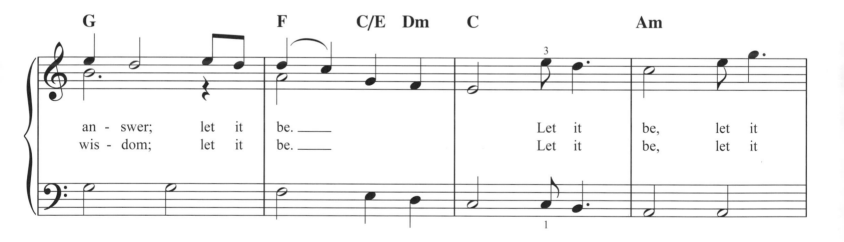

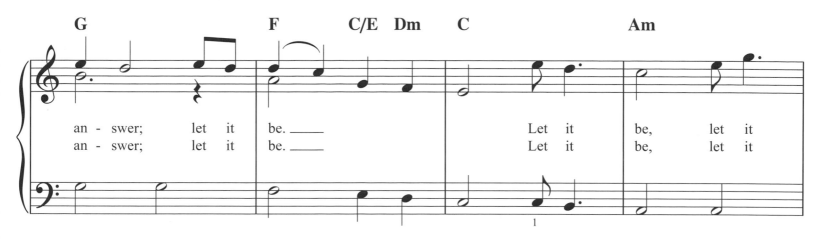

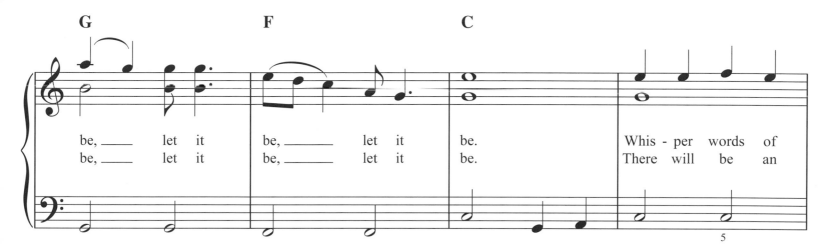

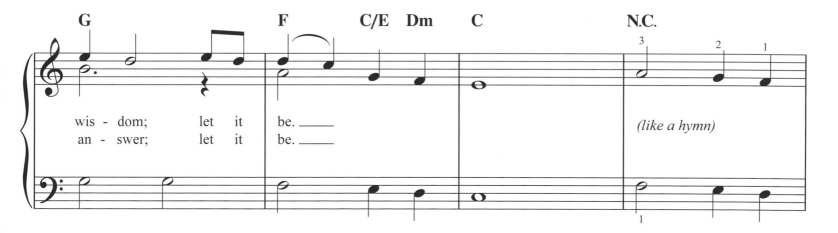

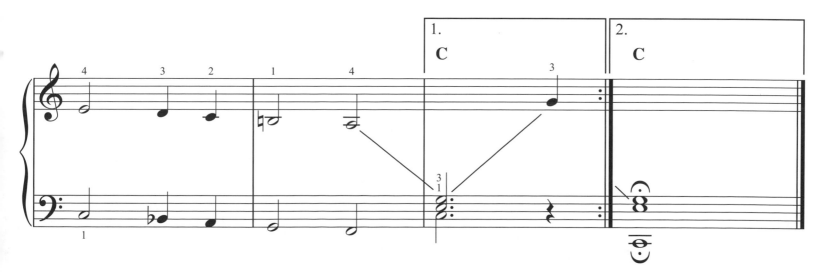

LOVE ME DO

Words and Music by JOHN LENNON
and PAUL McCARTNEY

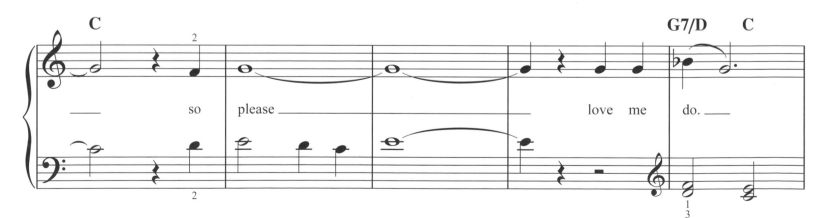

Love, love me do, ___ you know I love you, ___ I'll al - ways be true, ___ ___ so please ___ love me do. ___

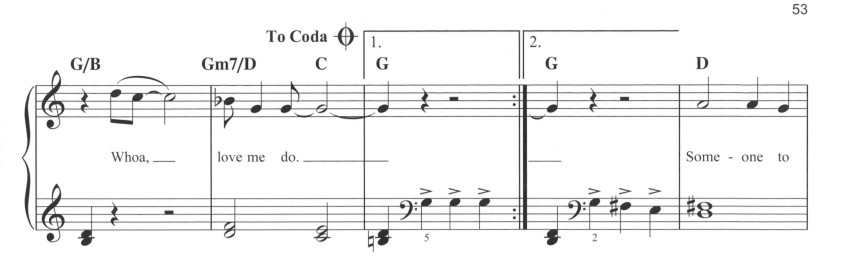

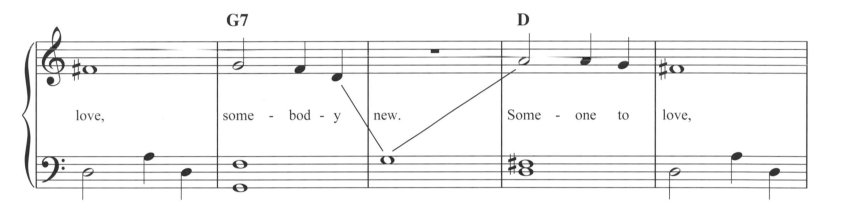

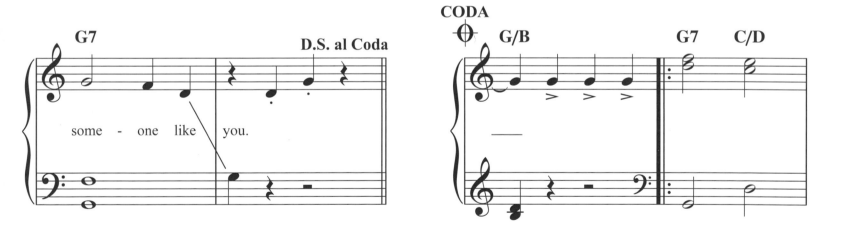

OCTOPUS'S GARDEN

Words and Music by
RICHARD STARKEY

I'd like to be
We would be warm

un - der the sea
be - low the storm

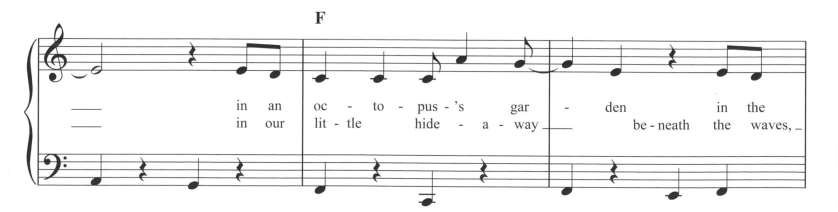

in an oc - to - pus's - gar - den in the
in our lit - tle hide - a - way be - neath the waves,

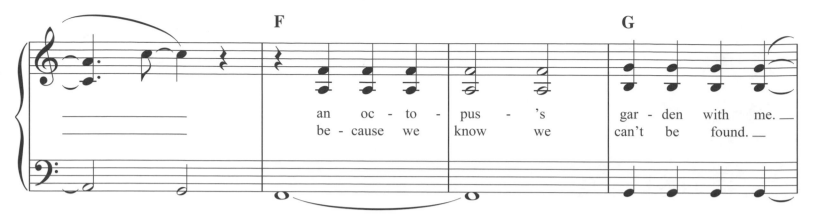

an oc - to - pus - 's gar - den with me.
be - cause we know we can't be found.

I'd like to be un - der the sea

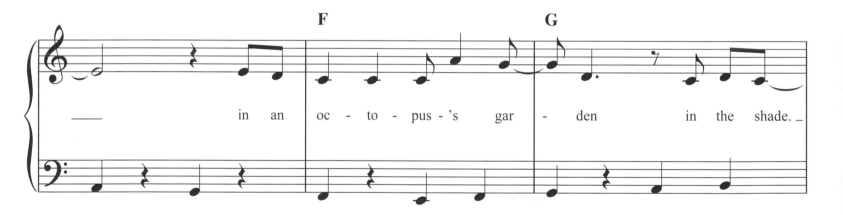

in an oc - to - pus - 's gar - den in the shade.

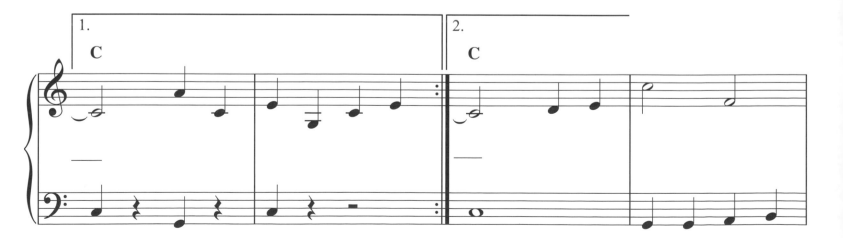

We would shout ___ and swim a - bout ___

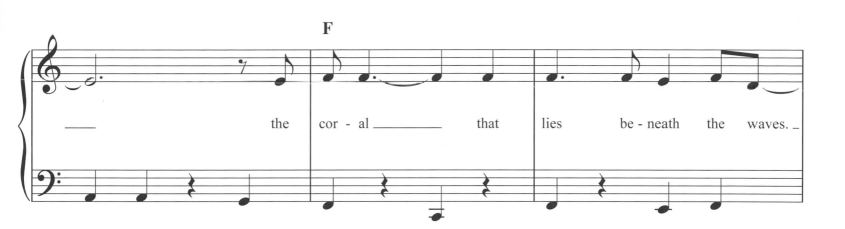

___ the cor - al ___ that lies be - neath the waves. ___

___ Oh, what joy ___ for

ev - 'ry girl and boy ___ know - ing ___ they're

hap - py   and they're   safe.   We would

be   so   hap - py   you   and   me;

no   one   there   to   tell   us   what   to   do.

I'd   like   to   be

under the sea ___ in an oc - to - pus - 's gar -

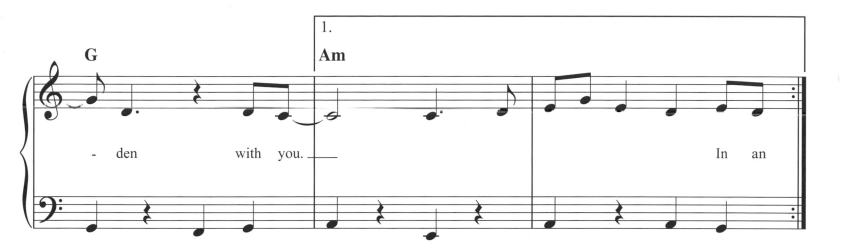

1.

- den with you. ___ In an

2.

___ In an oc - to - pus - 's gar -

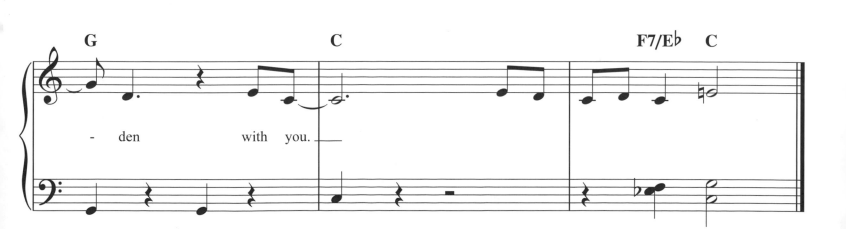

- den with you. ___

PENNY LANE

Words and Music by JOHN LENNON
and PAUL McCARTNEY

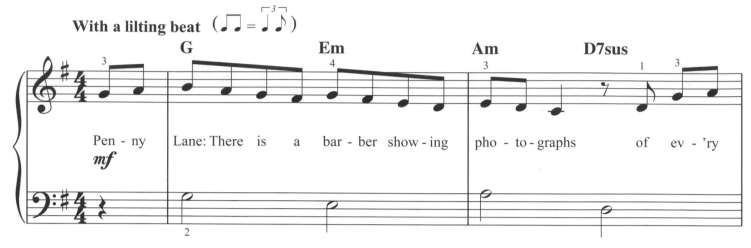

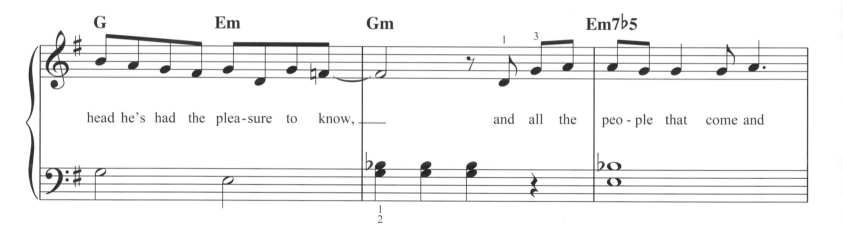

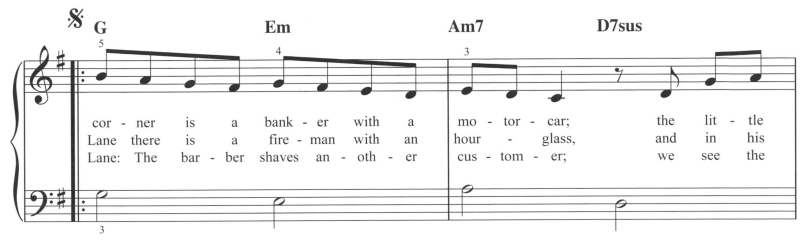

corner is a bank-er with a mo-tor-car; the lit-tle
Lane there is a fire-man with an hour - glass, and in his
Lane: The bar-ber shaves an-oth-er cus-tom-er; we see the

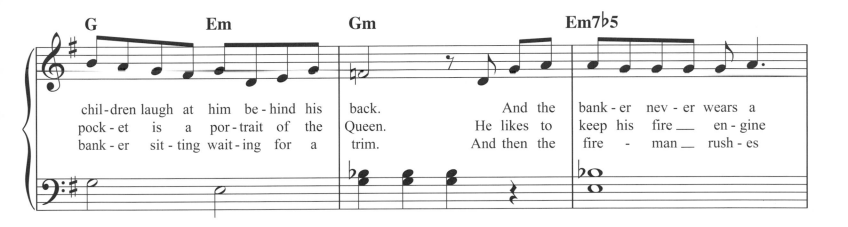

chil-dren laugh at him be-hind his back. And the bank-er nev-er wears a
pock-et is a por-trait of the Queen. He likes to keep his fire ___ en-gine
bank-er sit-ting wait-ing for a trim. And then the fire - man ___ rush-es

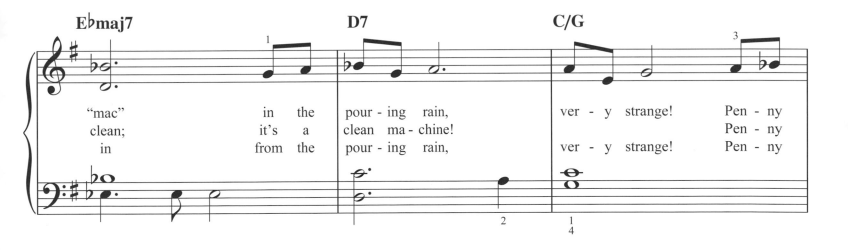

"mac" in the pour-ing rain, ver-y strange! Pen - ny
clean; it's a clean ma-chine! Pen - ny
in from the pour-ing rain, ver-y strange! Pen - ny

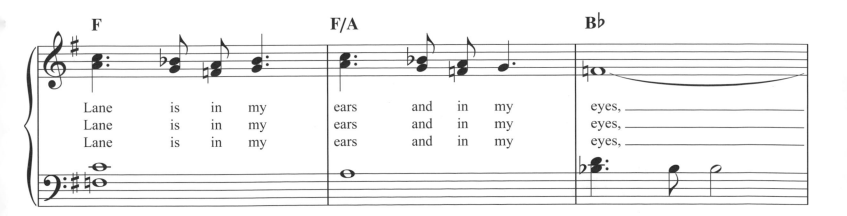

Lane is in my ears and in my eyes, ___
Lane is in my ears and in my eyes, ___
Lane is in my ears and in my eyes, ___

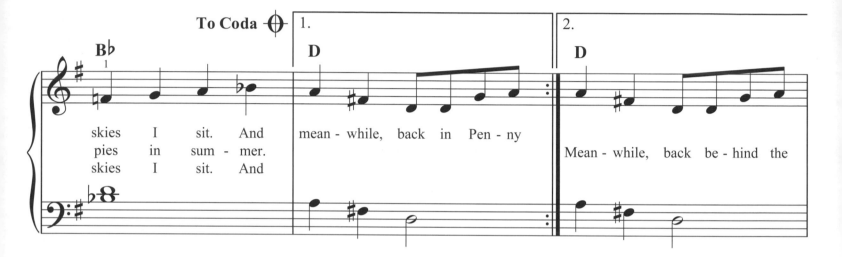

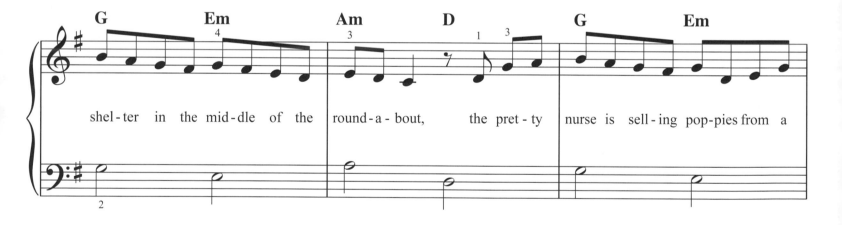

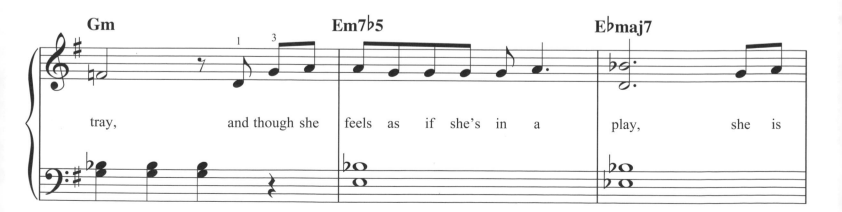

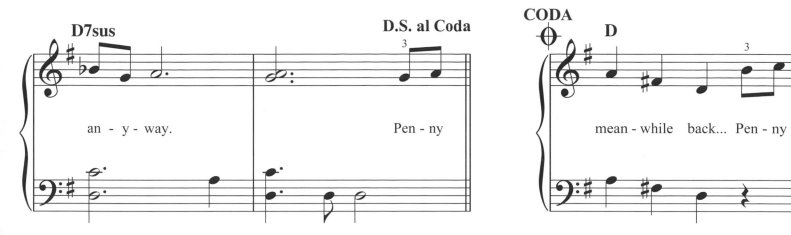

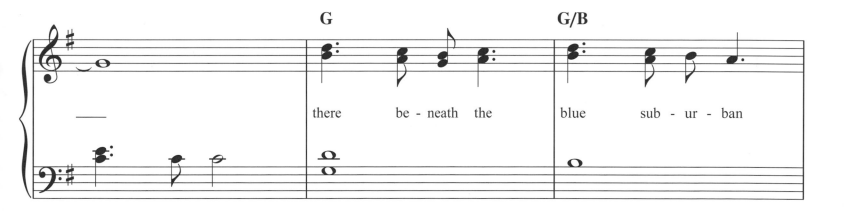

WHEN I'M SIXTY-FOUR

Words and Music by JOHN LENNON
and PAUL McCARTNEY

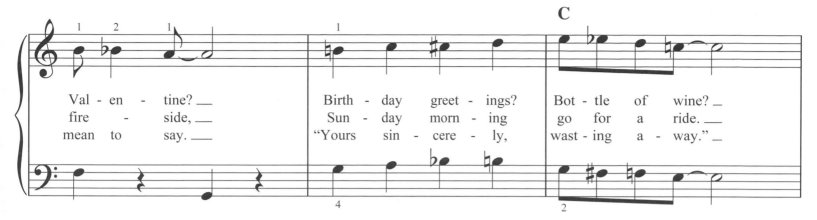

Val - en - tine? ___
fire - side, ___
mean to say. ___

Birth - day greet - ings?
Sun - day morn - ing
"Yours sin - cere - ly,

C
Bot - tle of wine? ___
go for a ride. ___
wast - ing a - way." ___

If I'd been out ___ till
Do - ing the gar - den,
Give me your an - swer,

quar - ter to three, ___
dig - ging the weeds, ___
fill in a form, ___

C7
would you lock the
who could ask for
mine for - ev - er -

F
door?
more.
more.

F#dim7
Will you still need ___ me,
Will you still need ___ me,
Will you still need ___ me,

C/G
will you still feed ___ me
will you still feed ___ me
will you still feed ___ me

A7/G **D7/F#**
when I'm
when I'm
when I'm

G7/F
six - ty -
six - ty -
six - ty -

To Coda ⊕

66

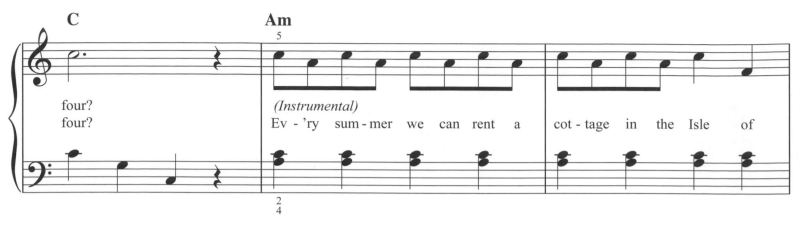

C　　　　　　　　　Am

four?
four?　　　　(Instrumental)
　　　　Ev - 'ry sum - mer we can rent a　　cot - tage in the Isle of

G/B　　　　　　　　Am

Wight if it's not too　　(Instrumental ends) dear.　　You'll　　　　be
　　　　　　　　　　　　　　　　　　　　　　We　　shall

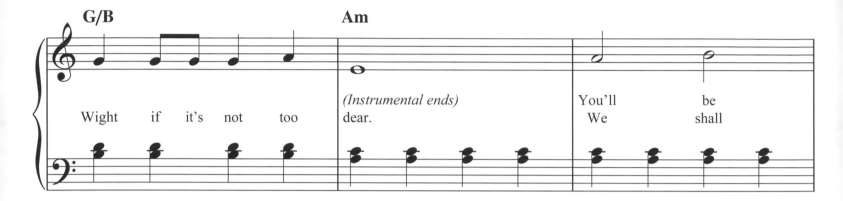

E/G♯　Am　E/G♯　Am　E/G♯　Am

old - er,　　　　too. _____
scrimp　　and　　save. _____

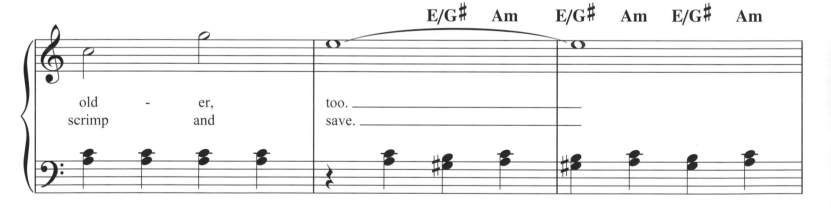

Dm/F

Ah, _____　　and　　　　if you　　say　　the　word __
Ah, _____　　grand - chil - dren　on　　your　knee, __

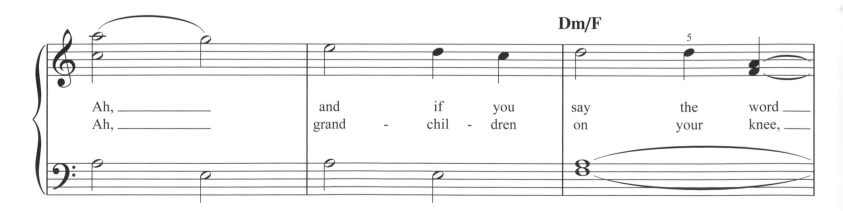

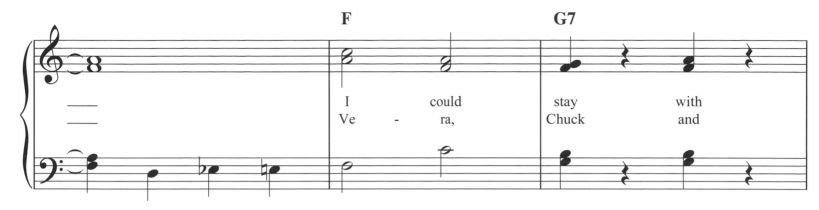

I could stay with
Ve - ra, Chuck and

you.
Dave.

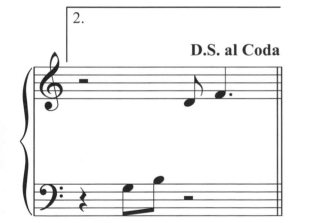

four?

WITH A LITTLE HELP FROM MY FRIENDS

Words and Music by JOHN LENNON
and PAUL McCARTNEY

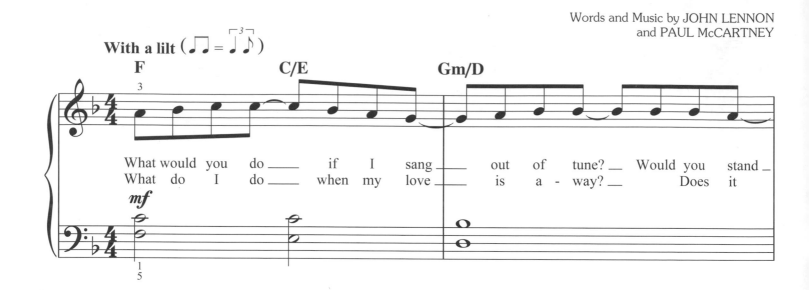

What would you do ___ if I sang ___ out of tune? ___ Would you stand ___
What do I do ___ when my love ___ is a-way? ___ Does it

___ up and walk ___ out on me? ___ Lend me your ears ___ and I'll sing ___
wor-ry you to be ___ a-lone? ___ How do I feel ___ by the end ___

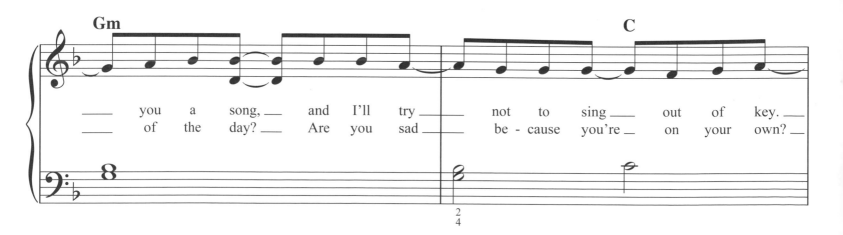

___ you a song, ___ and I'll try ___ not to sing ___ out of key. ___
___ of the day? ___ Are you sad ___ be-cause you're ___ on your own? ___

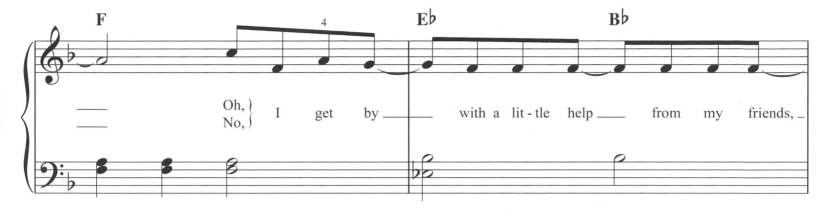

Oh, } I get by ____ with a lit-tle help ____ from my friends, ___
No, }

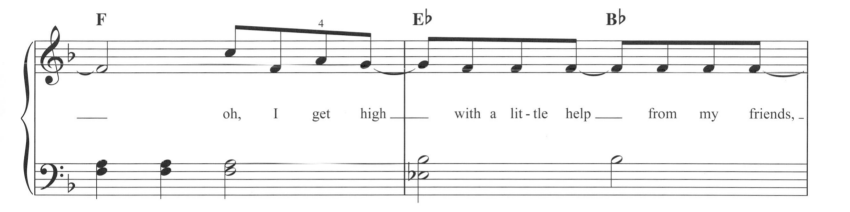

oh, I get high ____ with a lit-tle help ____ from my friends, ___

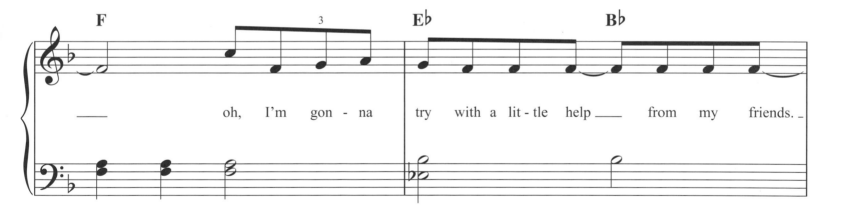

oh, I'm gon-na try with a lit-tle help ____ from my friends. ___

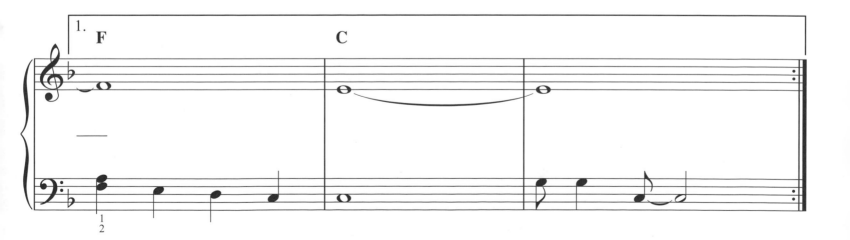

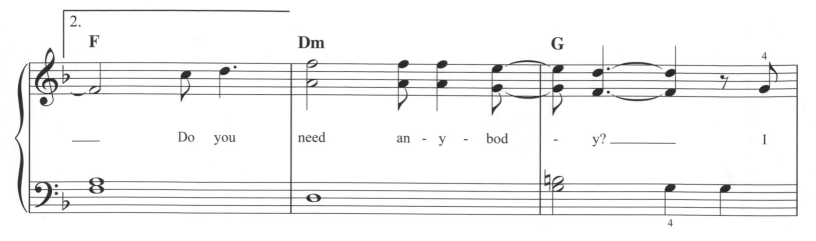

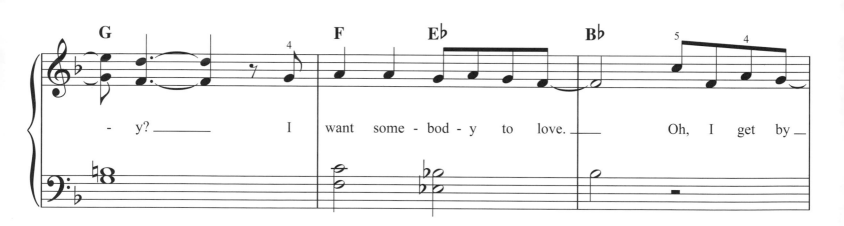

try with a lit-tle help ___ from my friends, ___ yes, I get high ___

___ with a lit-tle help ___ from my friends, ___ oh, I get by ___

___ with a lit-tle help ___ from my friends, ___ with a lit-tle help ___ from my friends! ___

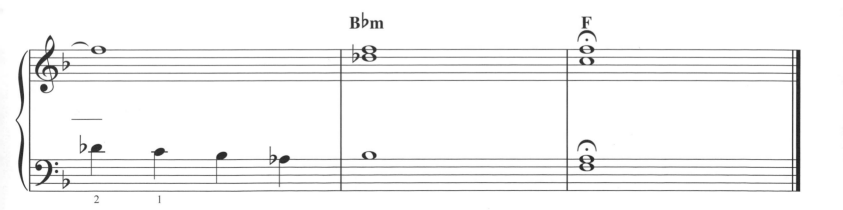

YELLOW SUBMARINE

Words and Music by JOHN LENNON
and PAUL McCARTNEY

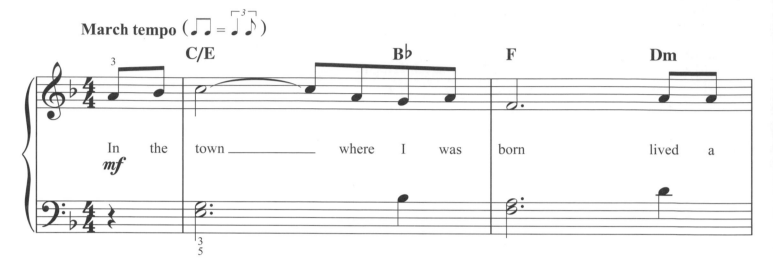

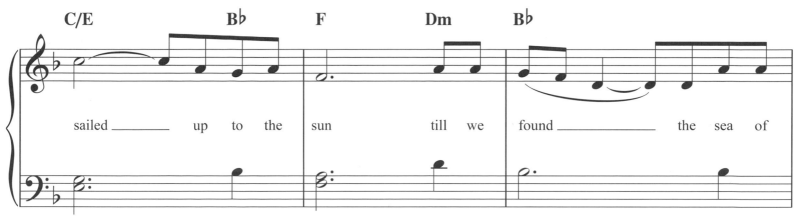

sailed _____ up to the sun till we found _____ the sea of

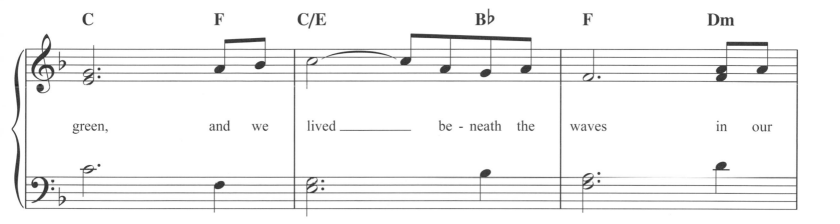

green, and we lived _____ be - neath the waves in our

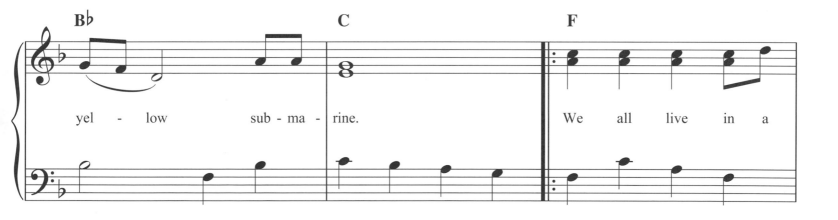

yel - low sub - ma - rine. We all live in a

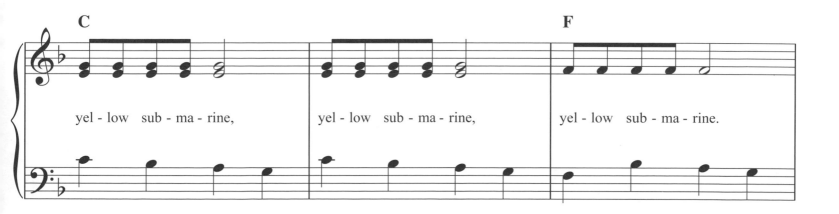

yel - low sub - ma - rine, yel - low sub - ma - rine, yel - low sub - ma - rine.

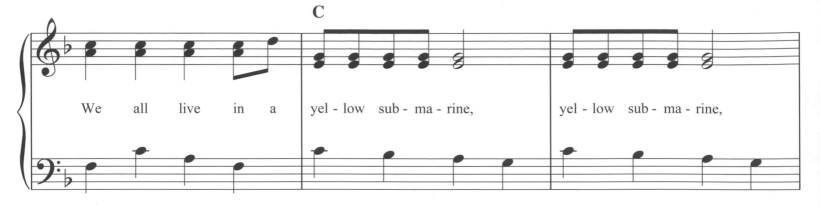

We all live in a yel - low sub - ma - rine,   yel - low sub - ma - rine,

yel - low sub - ma - rine. {And our   friends _____ are all on   board,   man - y
                             {As we   live _____ a life of   ease,   ev - 'ry

more of them _____ live next   door.   And the   band _____ be - gins to
one of us _____ has all we   need.   Sky of   blue _____ and sea of

1.

play:

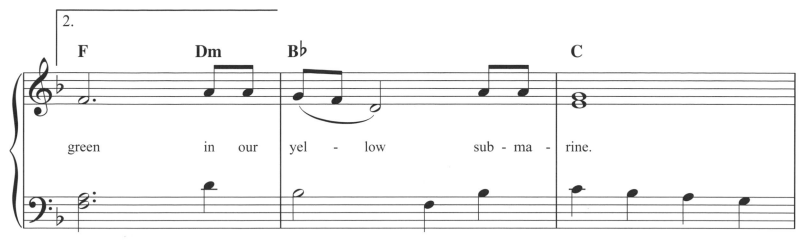

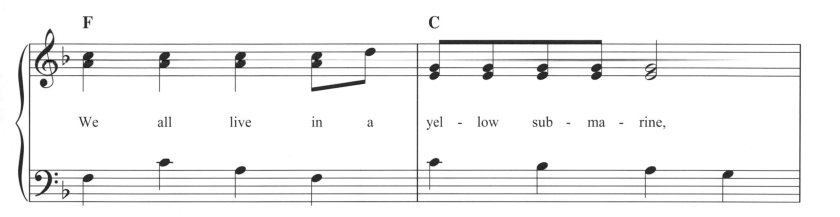

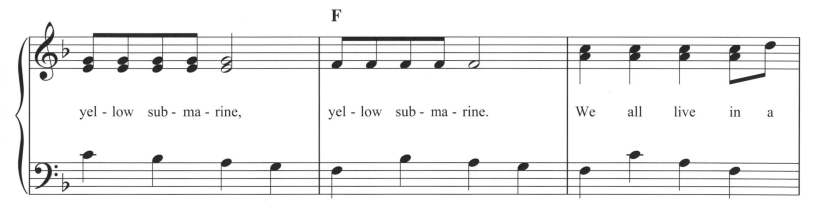

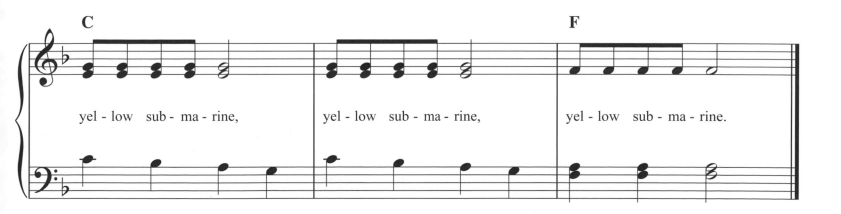

YESTERDAY

Words and Music by JOHN LENNON
and PAUL McCARTNEY

Moderately, with expression

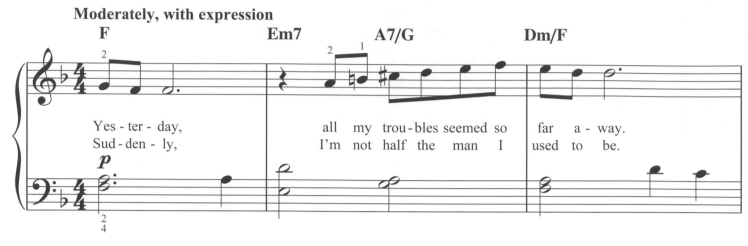

Yes - ter - day, all my trou - bles seemed so far a - way.
Sud - den - ly, I'm not half the man I used to be.

Now it looks as though they're here to stay. __ Oh, I be - lieve __ in
There's a shad - ow hang - ing o - ver me. __ Oh, yes - ter - day __ came

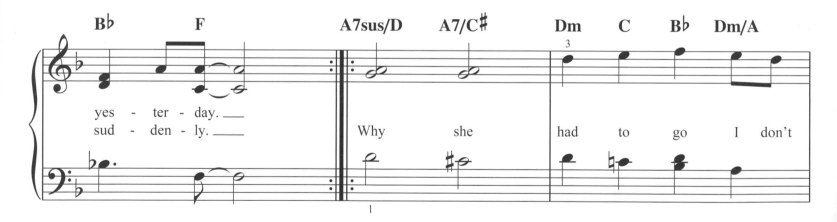

yes - ter - day. __
sud - den - ly. __ Why she had to go I don't

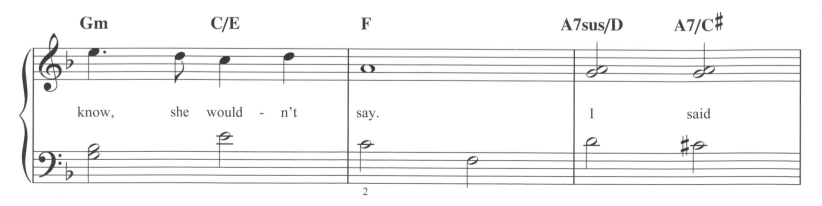

know, she would - n't say. I said

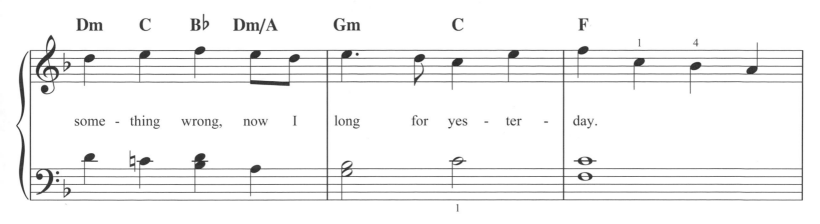

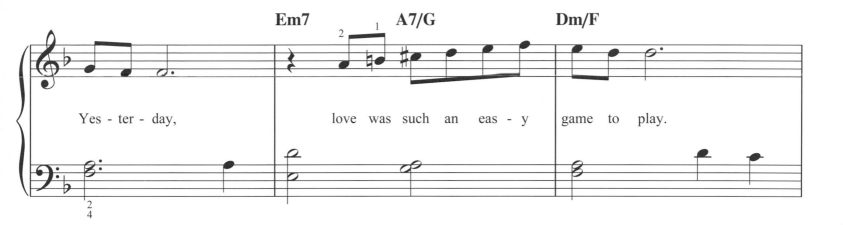

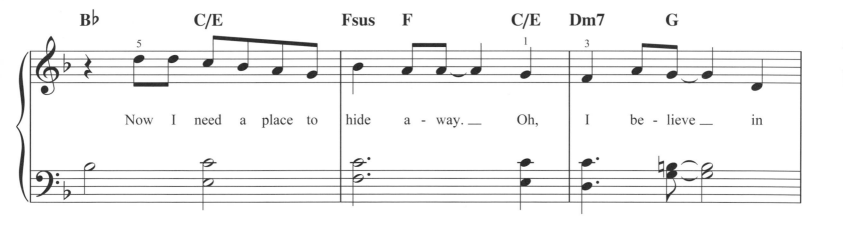

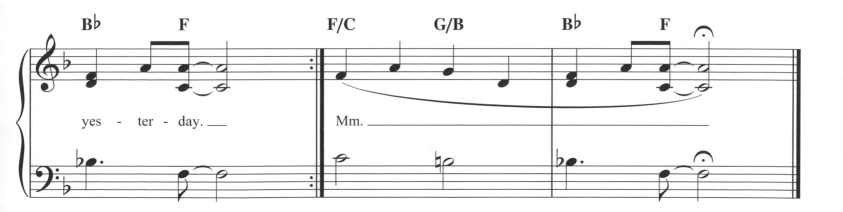

SOMETHING

Words and Music by
GEORGE HARRISON

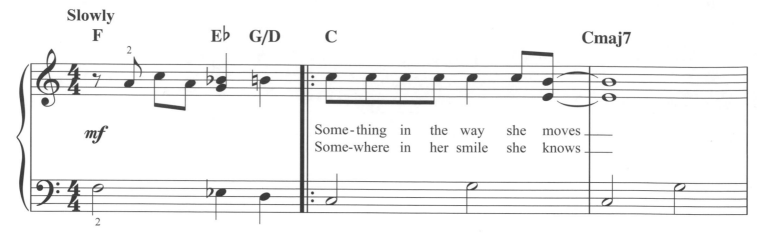

Some-thing in the way she moves ___
Some-where in her smile she knows ___

at - tracts me like no oth - er lov - er, _____ some-thing in the way she
that I don't need no oth - er lov - er, _____ some-thing in her style that

woos ___ me.
shows ___ me. }
I don't want to leave ___ her now, you

know I be - lieve ___ and how. ___

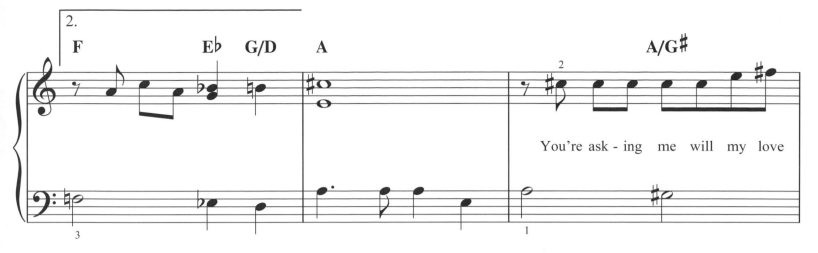

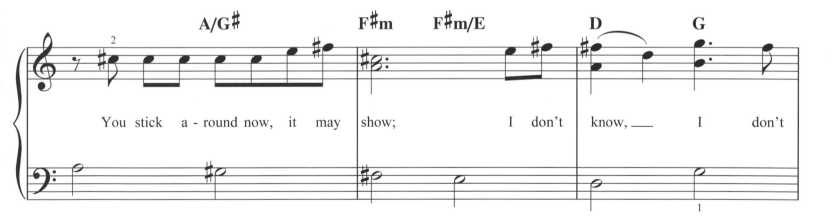

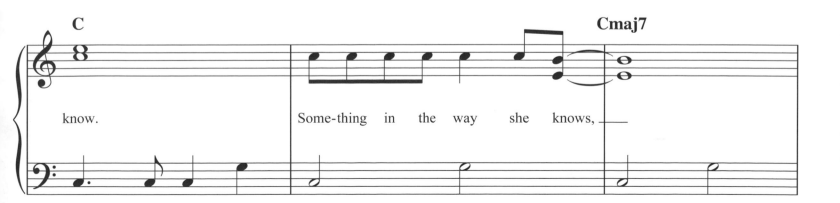

and all I have to do is think of her, some-thing in the things she

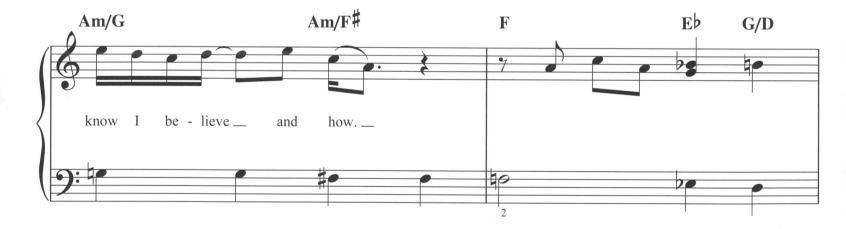

shows __ me. I don't want to leave __ her now, you

know I be - lieve __ and how. __

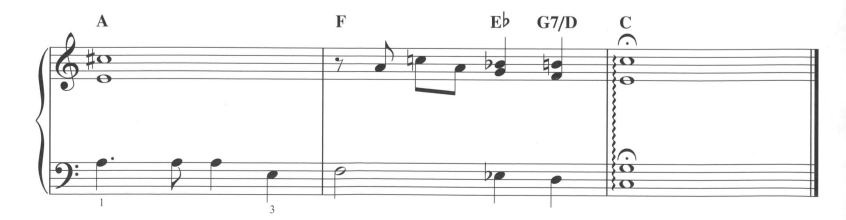